Bug Books
ANT

**Karen Hartley
and Chris Macro**

Heinemann
LIBRARY

First published in Great Britain by Heinemann Library
Halley Court, Jordan Hill, Oxford OX2 8EJ
a division of Reed Educational and Professional Publishing Ltd.
Heinemann is a registered trademark of Reed Educational & Professional Publishing Limited.

OXFORD MELBOURNE AUCKLAND
JOHANNESBURG BLANTYRE GABORONE
IBADAN PORTSMOUTH NH CHICAGO

Designed by Celia Floyd
Illustrations by Alan Male
Printed in Hong Kong/China

04 03 02 01 00
10 9 8 7 6 5 4 3 2 1

ISBN 0 431 01662 3
This book is also available in hardback (ISBN 0 431 01657 7).

British Library Cataloguing in Publication Data

Hartley, Karen
    Ant. - (Bug books) (Take-off!)
    1. Ants - Juvenile literature
    I.Title II. Macro, Chris
    595.7'96

Acknowledgements

The Publishers would like to thank the following for permission to reproduce photographs:
Heather Angel: p26; Ardea London Ltd: J Mason p7, Bruce Coleman Ltd: J Taylor p6, K Taylor pp10, 29; FLPA: M Thomas pp4, 9, 13; Garden Matters: P Goetgheluck p11, C Milkins p12; Nature Photographers Ltd: N Callow pp20, 22, 27; NHPA: N Callow pp14, 15, 25, S Dalton p24, E Janes p21, E Soder p23; Oxford Scientific Films: K Atkinson p8, A Butler p17, C Milkins pp16, 19; Papilio Photographic: p28; Premaphotos: K Preston-Mafham pp5, 18

Cover photograph reproduced with permission of Oxford Scientific Films/John Brown

Our thanks to Sue Graves and Stephanie Byars for their advice and expertise in the preparation of this book.

Every effort has been made to contact copyright holders of any material reproduced in this book. Any omissions will be rectified in subsequent printings if notice is given to the Publisher.

For more information about Heinemann Library books, or to order, please telephone +44 (0)1865 888066, or send a fax to +44 (0)1865 314091. You can visit our website at www.heinemann.co.uk

Any words appearing in the text in bold, **like this**, are explained in the Glossary.

Contents

What are ants? 4

What do ants look like? 6

How big are ants? 8

How are ants born? 10

How do ants grow? 12

What do ants eat? 14

Which animals attack ants? 16

Where do ants live? 18

What do ants do? 20

How do ants move? 22

How long do ants live? 24

How are ants special? 26

Thinking about ants 28

Bug map 30

Glossary 31

Index 32

What are ants?

Ants are small insects with six legs.

Ants are very small **insects**. They are found all over the world. Hundreds of ants live together in a group called a **colony**. Each colony makes a nest.

worker ant   male ant

The male ants have wings but the worker ants do not.

There are different kinds of ants in each nest. There are a few **queen** ants, male ants and many **workers**. The queen and the male ants have wings for part of their life.

What do ants look like?

Some ants are green like these.

Ants can be different colours. Some can be a pale yellow colour. Some are green. Most ants are black or brown. They are the ones we are going to find out about in this book.

There are over 6000 kinds of ants in the world.

head

eye

feeler

leg

Ants have six legs, two eyes and two feelers.

Ants have six legs. Each leg has **joints** and two small **claws** at the end. Ants have two eyes but they cannot see very well. They have two **feelers**. They use their feelers for touching and smelling.

How big are ants?

Big ants live in hot countries.

In hot countries, there are some very big ants. This ant is very big. It is nearly half as long as your middle finger. The black garden ants that live in **Europe** are very small.

The **queen** ant is bigger than the male ants. The **workers** are the smallest ants. They are half as big as the queen. Ants are small but very strong.

These small ants like to eat worms.

How are ants born ?

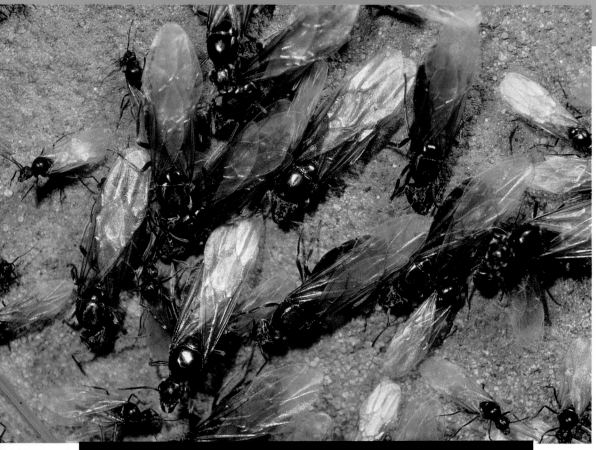

These male ants and queen ants are ready to mate.

When it is time to **mate** and start new nests, the young **queens** and male ants fly off together. Once the male ants have mated they die. The queen ants are now ready to start their new nests.

After mating the queen ants lose their wings.

eggs

The queen ant lays eggs in the soil. These eggs produce **worker** ants. When the workers **hatch**, they look after the queen ant and build the nest.

How do ants grow?

worker
ant

larva

One larva has already made its cocoon.

cocoon

A few days after the eggs are laid, a **larva hatches** from each egg. After about eight days the larva makes a **cocoon** around its body. The cocoon is quite hard so that it will protect the larva.

Worker ants move the eggs around the nest to keep them in the best places.

Inside the cocoon the larva is turning into a **pupa**. This takes three weeks. When the pupa is ready **workers** cut open the cocoon. Now the new ant is ready to come out.

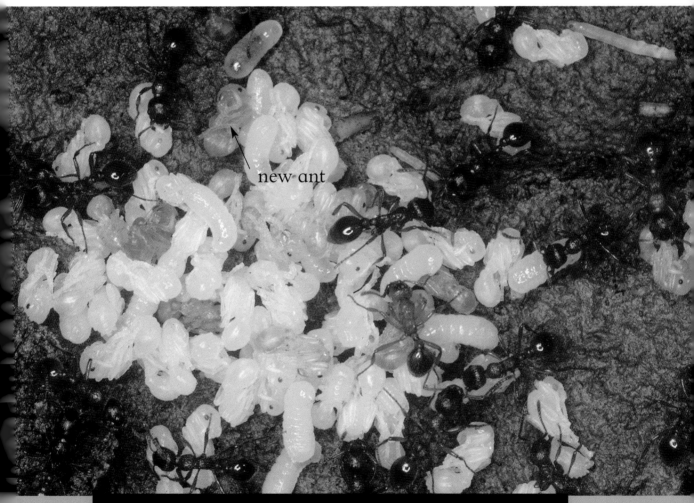

new ant

Workers cut open the cocoons to let out the new ants.

What do ants eat?

greenfly

These ants are drinking honeydew from greenflies.

Ants like to drink **honeydew**. They get honeydew from greenflies. Honeydew is very sweet. Ants stroke the greenflies with their **feelers**. This makes tiny drops of honeydew come out.

14

Most ants like sweet things. They eat fruit and seeds or even biscuits and jam if they are left around! They also eat worms, caterpillars and other **insects**.

This ant has found some tasty food!

Which animals attack ants?

Some beetles and other **insects** eat ants. **Workers** are always watching for any enemies that might attack them.

These ants are attacking each other.

A bird called the ant-thrush eats ants as its main food. Other birds and frogs eat ants too. Spiders eat ants if they catch them in their webs. In some countries animals called anteaters eat ants.

This bird has caught ants to eat.

Where do ants live?

Ants choose safe, warm places to build their nests.

Ants make their nests in places where they feel safe and warm. Some build their nests underground. Others make nests in old logs or under stones and rocks.

Ants make their nests as safe as possible. Ants that live in woods put pieces of wood on top of their nests. Others use soil to keep them safe. Ants' nests have many tunnels and little rooms.

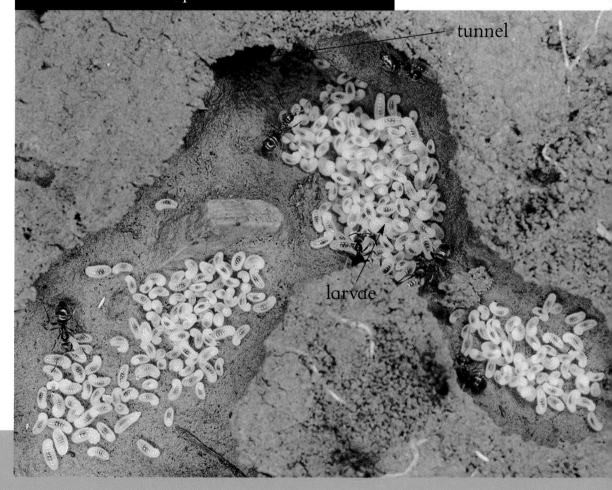

This ant nest has special rooms for **larvae**.

tunnel

larvae

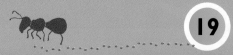

What do ants do?

This ant is busy now that the weather is warmer.

When the weather is cold the ants sleep in their nests. When the weather is warmer the **worker** ants are very busy. They work to look after the **colony**. They build the nest and keep it tidy.

20

These worker ants are looking after the eggs and the cocoons.

The workers have many jobs. They keep the eggs clean by licking them. They also collect food, feed the **larvae** and look after the **queen** and the **cocoons**.

21

How do ants move?

These ants are carrying big pieces of food back to their nest.

Ants are very busy and so they move very quickly. They can carry big pieces of food back to the nest. Some ants, like army ants and driver ants, follow each other in lines.

Ants use the **claws** on the end of their legs to help them climb. Some ants can also fly. In the summer, the **queen** ants and male ants fly when they are ready to **mate**. **Workers** do not fly.

These ants are using their claws to climb.

How long do ants live?

The worker ants protect the queen.

The **queen** ant lives the longest of all the ants in the **colony**. She might live for ten or fifteen years. The queen is kept safe in a special room in the nest. The **workers** protect the queen because she has an important job to do.

The male ants only live for a few months. They die after they have **mated** with the queen. The workers will live for about five years.

Worker ants like these will live for about five years.

How are ants special?

Ants work together to get jobs done.

Ants live and work together and help each other. Ants give off smells which other ants follow.

feeler

These ants are using their feelers to smell each other.

Ants have very special **feelers**. They use their feelers to tell them where they are going. Ants touch each other with their feelers. The smell tells them if an ant is a friend or an enemy.

Thinking about ants

Now you have read about ants can you answer
these questions?

1   Look at the ants' nest above. What different
     jobs do you think the ants are doing?

Look at the part of the ants' nest below.

2   Which is a **larva**? Is it A or B?

3   Which is a **cocoon**? Is it A or B?

4   Does the larva stage, or the cocoon stage
    come first?

5   What would you see when the cocoon
    breaks open?

Which ants look after the young?

A

B

Bug map

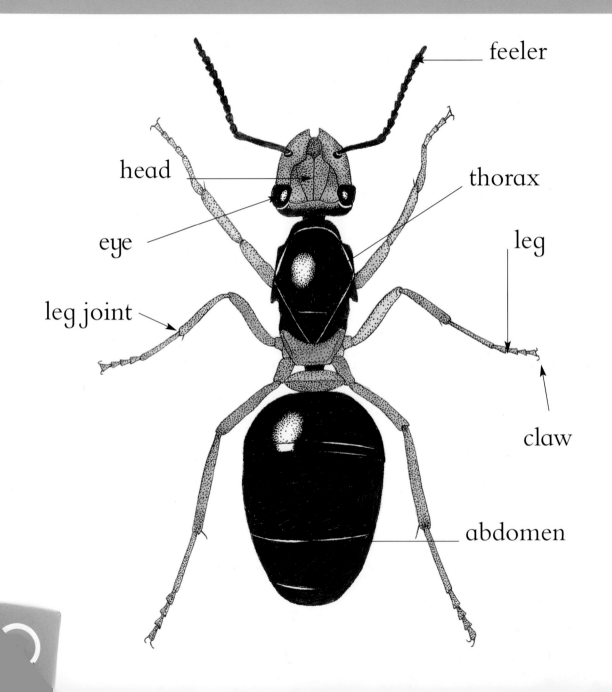

feeler

head

thorax

eye

leg

leg joint

claw

abdomen

Glossary

claws   sharp, bent points at the end of the legs. Claws are used for tearing or holding things

cocoon   the casing that grows round the larva

colony   a group of insects that live together

Europe   the United Kingdom, France and Spain are part of Europe

feelers   two long thin tubes that stick out from the head of an insect. They may be used to feel, smell or hear

hatch   to come out of an egg or cocoon

honeydew   the sweet liquid made by greenflies

insect   a small creature with six legs

joint   the part of a leg where it can bend

larva   (more than one = **larvae**) the little white grub that hatches from the egg

mate   a male and female ant mate to make baby ants

pupa   (more than one = **pupae**) older larva. The adult ant grows inside it

queen   mother ant

workers   ants that do all the work

Index

cocoon   12, 13, 21, 29

colony   4, 5

eggs   11, 12, 21

enemies   16, 17, 27

feelers   7, 14, 27, 30

flying   10, 23

food   14, 15, 21, 22

hatching   11, 12

larva   12, 13, 21, 29

male ant   5, 9, 10, 23, 25

mating   10, 25

nest   4, 10, 11, 18, 19, 20, 22, 28, 29

pupa   13

queen ant   5, 9, 10, 11, 21, 23, 24, 25

tunnels   19,

wings   5, 10

workers   5, 9, 13, 16, 20, 21, 23, 24, 25